CASA
ROCCA PICCOLA
Valletta

VIGOR ET LABOR

NICHOLAS DE PIRO

PHOTOGRAPHY
DANIEL CILIA

HERITAGE BOOKS

HOW TO GET TO CASA ROCCA PICCOLA

Casa Rocca Piccola is situated in the heart of Valletta.

It is easily reached by foot and is found on Republic Street just after Palace Square, the Grand Masters' Palace (the House of Parliament).

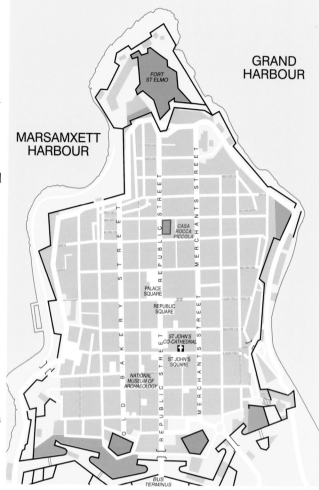

Casa Rocca Piccola
74 Republic Street
Valletta
Tel: 2122 1499

www.casaroccapiccola.com

Insight Heritage Guides Series No: 6
General Editor: Louis J. Scerri

Published by Heritage Books, a subsidiary of Midsea Books Ltd, Carmelites Street, Sta Venera HMR 11, Malta

Insight Heritage Guides is a series of books intended to give an insight into aspects and sites of Malta's rich heritage, culture and traditions.

Produced by Mizzi Design & Graphic Services
Printed by Gutenberg Press

First published 2004
This edition 2009

ISBN: 99932-39-88-7

CASA ROCCA PICCOLA, VALLETTA

Casa Rocca Piccola is the lived-in home of the de Piro family – an ancient Maltese lineage. The history of Casa Rocca Piccola goes back over 400 years to an era in which the Knights of St John, having successfully fought off the invading Turks in 1565, decided to build themselves a prestigious city to rival European capitals. Palaces were designed for prestige and aesthetic beauty in most of Valletta's carefully planned streets, and great bastion walls fortified the new sixteenth-century city.

The house is named after the first owner, Don Pietro La Rocca, admiral of the Order of St John in the Langue of Italy. It was, in later years, let to a succession of Italian aristocratic knights and was sold to a Maltese nobleman in the second half of the eighteenth century. What we are about to see is a house that has been lived in by Maltese families for over 200 years. It is now the home of the 9th Marquis de Piro

and his family. The Marquis is also 9th Baron of the Maltese fiefdom of Budach and a knight of Malta. Frances, the Marchioness, is English. They have four children: Cosmo, Clement, Louisa (Mrs Hugh Preston), and Anton. Their three young grandchildren are Serafina, Nicholas, and Mary Benedicta.

Casa Rocca Piccola houses a little museum called Costumes & Collections which is worth a visit. There are also the World War II shelters deep underground, cut out of the rock foundation of Valletta. They give you an idea of how people lived during the bombing of Malta. There is also a cafeteria in the old kitchens of the house.

A visit to Casa Rocca Piccola is an opportunity to see inside one of the last private unconverted Valletta palaces still lived in today. Let us climb the marble staircase and approach twelve principal rooms on the first floor – the *piano nobile*.

Pope Clement XI by Carlo Maratta

Right: **A Maltese 16th century credenza**

The *Sala Grande*

Vincenzo de Piro (detail)

THE SALA GRANDE

The Sala Grande is the tallest room in the house. The chest with the Maltese crosses is reputed to be the earliest surviving piece of Maltese domestic furniture and dates to the early 1500s. The chandelier is from Bohemia. It was made for candles and dates to the late eighteenth century.

On the pink and mustard-coloured walls hang some significant paintings.

The two portraits of popes are of Clement XI (left) and Clement XIV, both of whom bestowed important ecclesiastical privileges on the Maltese clergy. Clement XI was a member of the famous Albani family of Rome. He is painted here by Carlo Maratta. The de Piro family lent money to the Albanis in the early eighteenth-century. Other pictures of interest are the self-portrait of the court painter Antoine Favray (1706-98) signed and dated in Constantinople in 1763. The elegant Maltese lady with the wimple hanging over the inlaid roll-top desk is said to be a member of the Sceberras family, a work attributed to Francesco Zahra (1710-73). The Flemish artist Willem Benson (flourished 1551-64) painted the *Madonna and Child* on panels. The picture of *St Paul the Hermit* is one of at least three Mattia Preti (1613-99) versions of the subject. There are period pictures of *St John the Baptist as patron of the Order of Malta*; an ex-voto of *Countess Fremeaux kneeling beside St Roch*; and *Vincenzo de Piro in armour as colonel of the Royal Sicilian Regiment*.

The large black-lacquer eighteenth century bureau is in fact a portable chapel. Its appearance, when shut, is not too religious; however, when open it becomes a fully-functioning

chapel with its own tabernacle, relics, and the way of the cross. The altar-front bears the coat-of-arms of a Maltese nobleman, Marquis Pandolfo Testaferrata de Noto (1736-1816). It is decorated with pictures of exotic birds and flora and also panels depicting St Francis Xavier in China and in the company of the Indians of Goa. Portable chapels could be moved into a bedroom so that a mother, immediately after giving birth, could be present at the baptism of her child. A portable chapel could also be transported to country residences for the summer season.

Left: **Willem Benson's Madonna**

Above: **Antoine Favray - self-portrait (detail)**

THE CHAPEL

The house chapel adjoins the Sala Grande. The Palladian structure is made of wood and painted to simulate marble. It came to the present family by descent from Paolo Sceberras Testaferrata and his wife Maria Angelica Perdicomati Bologna (brother and sister-in-law of Fabrizio, Malta's only cardinal). The altarpiece of the *Madonna and Child with San* Gaetano is by Pietro Paolo Caruana (1794-1852). The picture of *Our Lady of Sorrows* hanging below the picture of the *Crucifixion* is by Ignatius Stern (1680-1748). There are eighteenth-century pictures of *St Rita* and *St Lucy* and a recent watercolour of *Monsignor Joseph de Piro, founder of the Missionary Order of St Paul* by Matt Bruce, R.I. On show are some relics, chalices,

The Chapel

Chalice made in the Vatican for Fabrizio Sceberras Testaferrata (1757-1843), Malta's only Cardinal

papal buskins, and many other items of memorabilia including a silver statuette of St Quentin presented to Leo XIII – it left the Vatican collection during the reign of Pius X.

THE WINTER DINING ROOM

The table and chairs you see here are Florentine. The pair of landscapes are typical seventeenth-century Maltese in their original carved frames. The two *putti* represent young Cupid and Vulcan and are by Thomas Barker of Bath (1769-1847). Above the enfilade doors are two allegorical paintings representing *Love* and *Time*. The Pompeian decoration was designed and executed by Arthur Rose.

THE ARCHIVES

The Archivum de Piro comprises an extensive private family collection of documents and records. The de Piros apparently were not in Malta before the arrival of the knights of St John – they are thought to have accompanied them from Rhodes. The first locally-recorded de Piro wills

are from the 1500s. Grand Master Ramon Perellos ennobled the family with a barony in 1716 and later in 1742 Philip V of Spain bestowed the marquisate. The 1st Baron and 1st Marquis was a lawyer. He took charge of the family's business affairs which included dealings involving infidel slaves. There are surviving bills of lading as well as bills for transactions in which Giovanni Pio de Piro is selling Muslims to a Muslim trader called Raïs. There are hundreds of documents relating to the running of State palaces as well as the rest of his personal administration in Malta and overseas. He invested in land, ships, and cargoes of textiles, grain, sugar, rice, coffee, and cocoa. He lent money, quite often to knights of Malta including the illustrious Fra Carlo Albani, nephew of Pope Clement XI. Gio'Pio took on the responsibilities of Avola in Sicily from its principal landlord who lived in Spain, and he produced sugar, running the whole gamut of production from planting to processing and distributing.

***Opposite page:*
The Winter Dining Room

The Archivum de Piro and a detail of a manuscript

Lorenzo Ubaldesco de Piro's degree from the University of Messina, written in gold leaf

The Cabinet

the snake at St Paul's feet: this is to emphasise the story of his arrival in Malta described in the Acts of the Apostles. The legend is that since Paul was bitten, there have been no poisonous snakes on the islands.

THE CABINET

Here we find heraldic pictures including proofs of nobility which were necessary for joining the Order of St John. Normally four generations of noble blood were required before you could be admitted to the order. There are two showcases displaying chessmen. The majority of the pieces are ivory. Ask your guide to point out the Maltese sets. If you look carefully you can observe that the king is Christian and the queen has no crown. This perhaps illustrates the fact that the grand master of Malta was celibate, and therefore there was no 'queen' in Malta. The Chinese set includes George III of England and Hanover as the white king, while the Emperor of China is red.

In the various cupboards are seals, documents, and other items of interest including more than eight hundred first copies of letters sent by Gio'Pio.

On the table in the middle of the room is the carved wooden statue of St Paul, patron saint of Malta. This seventeenth-century carving is considered by some to be the model for the famous statue of *St Paul* by Melchiorre Gafà in the church of St Paul Shipwrecked in Valletta. Note

In this room is one of the principal

treasures of the house. It is the gilded sedan chair made for Frà Victor Nicolas de Vachon Belmont, a French Knight of Malta. He served as Captain General of the Galleys from 13 October 1764 to 9 January 1766. You can see his coat-of-arms on the front door of the vehicle. This chair, with its ornate painting and overall gold colour, coats-of-arms, banners, and plush interior was probably designed to show off the fact that it was presented by Grand Master Pinto (1741-73) to one of Malta's most senior knights.

In those days both freemen from the local population as well as Turkish or African slaves would have carried sedan chairs. It was apparently a popular job as there was a lot of waiting involved and the journeys were short. One advantage of this form of transport was that one could also be carried from one's drawing room into another palace drawing room (up and down the stairs too) without the inconvenience of actually stepping outside. The owner of this chair did not leave Malta with the banished knights in 1798, he decided to stay on in spite of Napoleon's orders. The British admired this Frenchman and, having found him penniless – he had sold his furniture to continue the charity work to which he was dedicated – he was awarded a small pension. De Vachon lived on until 1807 and was buried 'with pomp' at St John's Cathedral. His tombstone is in the Chapel of France.

THE FOUR-POSTER BEDROOM

The bed was Orsola de Piro d'Amico's matrimonial bed. She married in 1867 and gave birth to nine children: seven boys and two girls. All survived. Two became priests and one may yet be proclaimed a saint if his *causa* is successful.

The Heraldry cabinet

The Captain General of the Galley's sedan chair.

The shaving bowl to the right of the bed is eighteenth-century, and the chamber-pot below is Venetian blown glass and is also over two hundred years old.

The Pre-Raphaelite picture is perhaps of the Roman martyr St Rufina but it might also be simply symbolic of martyrdom. It was painted by the celebrated Maltese artist Giuseppe Calì (1846-1930), Marquis de Piro's great-grandfather. He decorated many churches including the interior of the rotunda at Mosta, the Church of St Francis in

Martyrdom by Giuseppe Calì

18th-century Neapolitan *Madonna and Child*

Valletta, and the Dominican church around the corner from this house. The other pictures are of the *Bambino of Aracœli* covered in jewellery, and the large *Madonna and Child* is from the studio of Francesco de Mura (1696-1782) of Naples. The picture of *St George and the Dragon* is on parchment. The hanging bedhead is early eighteenth-century.

THE GREEN ROOM

The portrait of Sir Giuseppe Maria de Piro, G.C.M.G., 4th Baron of Budach, is by Charles Allingham. The 4th Baron was the first Maltese to command a British regiment. His military commission hangs under his portrait. His wife, Antonia Moscati Gatto Xara, Baroness of Benwarrad, was also painted by Allingham. The small eighteenth-century portrait of the baby (this may have been a boy) has been attributed to Antoine Favray whose self-portrait you have

Fabrizio Sceberras Testaferrata, the only Maltese cardinal, was his elder brother. The portrait above is of a young Igino de Piro, 7th Baron of Budach. He is wearing his red British Army uniform. He fought at the famous Siege of Ladysmith in the South African Boer War of 1899-1901.

The colourful blown-glass chandelier is Venetian and was made for candles. The carved console tables are eighteenth-century Maltese. Their design is attributed to Francesco Zahra.

THE LIBRARY

Look above the doors and you will see the ten historic ship paintings. They were produced during the reign of Grand Master Jean-Paul Lascaris (1636-57). They are reputed to have decorated the *gran salone* aboard his ceremonioal barge. All the scenes are fantasy. Many Italian artists of the seventeenth century liked to paint imaginary scenes in order to produce a more dramatic or even romantic landscape.

seen in the Sala Grande. The Maltese gentleman in blue uniform to the right is General Michele Sceberras Testaferrata. He wears the Royal Bavarian Order of St George about his neck. The decoration was given to him by Maximilian I Joseph, first king of Bavaria. He was entrusted with the education of the crown prince and was chamberlain to the royal household.

Opposite page: The Green Room

Left: Maltese baby c.1770 attributed to Antoine Favray

The Lascaris bureau

The Library

Top: The Porphyry Room

Marchesa Francesca Xara

In the corner is a Maltese clock. It is early and very simple; it was made with only one hand indicating the time. This particular timepiece needs to be wound up three times a day. There are several portraits here including one of Sir Walter Scott who visited Malta in 1831 and a rare picture of Samuel Taylor Coleridge who was on the island from 1804. Ask your guide to point them out. A portrait of Grand Master Emanuel de Rohan Polduc (1775-97) and another of the last Grand Master to rule Malta, the German Ferdinand Hompesch (1797-98) who was ignominiously ousted by Napoleon in 1798. Between them is Cardinal Portocarrero who is considered a founding father of the National Library.

THE PORPHYRY ROOM

The ceiling is original – a surviving wooden *soffit* which is over 400 years old.

The bureau-bookcase with its fine marquetry is an outstanding example of seventeenth-century Maltese furniture. It bears the arms of the Lascaris family emphasized with *fleurs-de-lis*. Grand Master Lascaris was French. It is said that this bureau originally came from the state collection and was sold off at the time of the French occupation of Malta.

The portrait within an ornate *cartouche* is of Giovanni Pio (John Pius) who was created 1ˢᵗ Baron of Budach by Grand Master Raymòn Perellos y Roccaful (1697-1720) in 1716. Philip V of Spain conferred the title of Marquis de Piro on him in 1742. Look out for the mountain in the background of his portrait, it symbolises his connection with Sicily: it is Mount Etna. At varying times he was procurator of wheat for the Grand Master of Malta and also *segreto regio* of the King of Spain. To the

Portraits of *Grand Master Raymòn Perellos* (*top*) and *Giovanni Pio de Piro* (*above*)

left is a portrait of his father Lorenzo Ubaldesco (1646-1723) attributed to Mattia Preti. To the right of the 1st Baron is his son Antonio Felicissimo de Piro who died before his father and left an infant heir Vincenzo. On his grandfather's death, Vincenzo became 2nd Baron and 2nd Marquis. He was elected as a representative of the Maltese people against the French when they took over in 1798. He died in 1799 and his son Antonio's portrait, looking more than a little Nelsonian, is over the door leading to the dining-room.

The portrait of the little girl to the left of the window was painted in 1735. It depicts the child Marchesa Francesca Xara and was probably painted in connection with a marriage contract. The mountain in the background is symbolic of her family property in Sicily (we have no mountains in Malta). Her cheeks and hands have been painted to make her look chubby, a sign of health in the eighteenth century. She is also wearing a great deal of coral jewellery to protect her from the Evil Eye. The picture below is attributed to Mattia Preti towards the end of his life. It depicts Grand Master Perellos. Opposite, over the fireplace is the large canvas of St Nicasius who was an early martyr of the Order of St John. To the right is Edward Caruana Dingli's portrait of Igino de Piro, 7th Baron of Budach, who became president of the Malta Senate. To the right of the window is a portrait of Antonio Cassar Torregiani also by Caruana Dingli. He was the only businessman to own Casa Rocca Piccola in four hundred years. He founded The National Bank of Malta, was elected a senator, and was president of the Chamber of Commerce. His beautiful wife

Margaret was the daughter of the artist Giuseppe Calì. Antonio and Margaret were the parents of the present Dowager Baroness de Piro of Budach.

THE BLUE ROOM

The surgical implements under the glass top of the coffee table in the centre of the room are unique: they are the only doctor's instruments to have survived from the Hospitaller Order of St John in silver from the eighteenth century. They were made in the reign of the French Grand Master Manuel de Rohan. The velvet case is original. The Knights of Malta as well as being a military and a religious Order, were also very advanced in surgery. They could operate on a cataract of the eyes and also remove a gallstone. Their hospital housed the largest ward in Europe and could look after over 600 patients at any one time. All were served on silver.

There is some antique Maltese silver in the showcase. Look out for the coconut tobacco jars with the silver-gilt cockerel finials. The cockerel was the heraldic emblem of the noble family of Gargallo, one of whom was

Opposite page:
The Blue Room

The silver collection includes the only known example of a Maltese sponge box (*top*), a Maltese coffee pot (*above*) and tabacco jars (*below*)

a notorious bishop of Malta. The hand-hammered glove tray to the left is from the seventeenth century and the coffee pot gives us an idea of the elegant style predominant in the eighteenth century – both are of Maltese manufacture.

Perhaps one should observe the lovely baroque façade of St Catherine's Church visible through the window. When the doors of the church are open, it is possible to see the high altar.

THE SUMMER DINING-ROOM

This was once an open terrace overlooking the small garden. With the marble staircase, it is an *art nouveau* addition to the house. The table has been laid out with silver and china and Maltese lace. The tablemats are embroidered with the family coat-of-arms and the wine glasses are engraved with the family crest.

The large gilt mirror is Maltese and bears the arms of 'd'Amico Inguanez'.

The Carrara marble statue of the goddess Diana dominates the far end

The Summer Dining Room

of the room. The *trompe l'oeil* behind the statue produces an exaggerated perspective and gives the impression that the space is longer.

The matching portraits are by Edward Caruana Dingli (1876-1950) – they are of the 8th Baron and his Baroness, Philomena Cassar Torreggiani at the time of their marriage in 1938. On the other side of the room is a portrait of Monica de Piro, daughter of the 7th Baron of Budach, painted by Sir Harold Acton's father Arthur Acton in Florence in about 1931.

The series of pictures along the top of the long wall are by Doris Zinkeisen, some of whose work can be seen at the Tate Gallery. The modern pictures either side of the arch are by Evelyn Gibbs (left) and John Bratby (right).

THE STAIRCASE

The large murals were painted by Maltese artist Ramiro Calì (1884-1947). On the left is *Electricity* (observe the wires and electric bulb) and on the right *Agriculture*. The artist's beautiful sister Margaret was the lady of the house after 1918; she married Antonio Cassar Torreggiani, OBE, miller, banker, and entrepreneur. The portrait of the lady in a straw hat is of Marchioness de Piro by Mary de Piro. The watercolour by Arthur Bell is Louisa daughter of the house wearing the traditional faldetta. The engraving which includes a Maltese dog is by Sir Edwin Landseer (1802-73).

THE BOMB SHELTERS

Valletta and the surrounding harbour areas were among the most heavily bombed areas of Europe in World War II. In April 1942, as many as 15 air raids a day hit the island and caused untold devastation. The people of Valletta took to seek shelter in the tunnels and wells under the city. However, much work was needed to improve access and enlarge the spaces under the city.

Because of the large size of Casa Rocca Piccola it has three wells, two of which were converted into bomb shelters in World War II. All were cut out of the solid rock foundation of Valletta and are part of the original quarry used to build the house 400 years ago.

Bomb Shelter 1: The first shelter you will see is the smaller of the two and could house about thirty people. You can see how it was strengthened with a concrete ceiling, steel beams, and

The quarry

a central column. It was designed to take a direct hit, and one must add that some bomb shelters did collapse under the force of bombs.

If you continue to follow the signs, you will be taken down to the larger shelter.

Bomb Shelter 2: Over here part of the concrete ceiling has been removed. You can see a cross-section of the construction if you look up. The area at the top was tightly packed with soil and stone chippings to soften the blast. If you look carefully around, you will see crosses on the walls. This is where people placed their beds and carved a cross above for protection. There is even one cross with a niche for a religious picture beneath it. About thirty people could sleep here and, when things got very busy, up to 150 people would cram into the shelter. Because this well was the largest in the area, it was used as a church on Sundays. People came in through the tunnels and a temporary wooden altar was set up for the service.

The lamps you see on the wall would have been lit with paraffin.

If you look around you can see different access points to the shelter. The others are all closed now. They used to connect to the hundreds of subterranean tunnels of Valletta. It is said that there are more streets under Valletta than on the surface.

The Family Shelter: Antonio Cassar Torregiani created this shelter in 1935 for his family and his servants. It was more of an emergency shelter to be used if anyone was in the house during an air raid. Thousands of people moved out of the city during the war but the ones who stayed either occupied in the large wells or created their own shelter like this one. As you leave the wells, you can enter this private shelter. You can see the zig-zag construction to hinder the blast of a bomb. This was the first bomb shelter built in Malta. If you walk right through, you will see the little room carved in the rock, and then farther on and around the corner you will end up in the little garden of Casa Rocca Piccola.

COSTUMES & COLLECTIONS

This area was created by excavating down to the foundations of the house. It displays many items collected and donated and is a tribute to the generosity of kind friends and relations who have passed on their old stored away paraphernalia to the Casa Rocca Collection.

Among the many rotated items in the collection are an exquisite blue velvet ball dress, a striped silk long coat, a nobleman's golden waistcoat, a buff-coloured silk dress with an outstanding *pettorino* or stomacher, all from the eighteenth century. There are items from the nineteenth century and even the twentieth. Costumes have to be moved around and put to rest regularly, therefore it is not possible to describe exactly what is on show at any one time. There are also wedding dresses, court dress, underwear, children's clothes, as well as a collection of hats, spectacles, walking sticks, pipes, snuff boxes, buckles, silver card cases, ivory lace bobbins, and more. This is a good glimpse of how the local gentry of the past were dressed. The lace collection is one of the finest on the island but items of both lace and costume are not always on show.

Maltese costumes from the 18th and 19th century

CASA ROCCA PICCOLA

Casa Rocca Piccola built in around 1580 is named after its first owner, Don Pietro La Rocca, admiral of the Order of St. John in the langue of Italy. On his death, he left the property to the langue of Italy. It was then let to a succession of high-ranking Italian knights of Malta, one of whom became bishop of Malta.

THE BALÌ OF NAPLES FRÀ FRANCESCO LANFREDUCCI c.1650

He died at Casa Rocca Piccola on 17 May 1656. An earli²er Lanfreducci was a hero of the Great Siege of Malta in 1565. The large palazzo of the Lanfreducci family was pulled down to make way for the nineteenth-century Roy²al Opera House. The present headquarters of the Malta Association of the Sov²er²eign Order of Malta was another Lanfreducci house.

CHEVALIER FRÀ GASPARE FERRO 1682

MONSIGNOR FRÀ GASPARE GORI MANCINI OF SIENA 1699

He was bishop of Malta from 1722 to 1728 during the reign of Grand Master Frà Anton Manoel de Vilhena. He is buried in the conventual church of St John, later renamed 'co-ca²the²dral'. The tabernacle door and altar front with a medallion depicting the martyrdom of St Catherine in the chapel of Italy of the same church were donated by him but later stolen by Napoleon.

CHEVALIER FRÀSCIPIONE MALASPINA 1727

CHEVALIER FRÀ FERDINANDO FILIGERI COMMENDATORE FRA BALDASSARE TORRES 1745

COMMENDATORE FRÀ GIO' ANTONIO LAMBERTI 1751

COMMENDATORE FRÀ GIUSEPPE PROVANA DA COLEGNO 1756

He is buried at St John's in Valletta.

COMMENDATORE FRÀ AMADEO BARALLA 1757

CHEVALIER FRA ALESSANDRO ROVIDA 1757

COMMENDATORE FRÀ SAVERIO AREZZO 1766

COMMENDATORE FRÀ ANDREA VENTURI 1772

COMMENDATORE ROVERE 1784

At a deliberation of the Italian Langue held on 16th November 1784, it was proposed to sell the house, and the premises were valued at 8,358 *scudi*; however, it was decided that the palazzo was not to be disposed of for less than 10,000 *scudi*. The langue of Italy sold the building to the head of a Maltese noble family.

GIO' FRANCESCO 2ND COUNT SANT 1788

He married Chiara Bonici Platamone Cassia 7th Baroness of Ghariexem and Tabia in her own right.

Gio Francesco purchased most of the property in this block which included Casa Rocca Grande (now split into two: Palazzo Messina and Palazzo Marina). An astute businessman and a survivor, he led the Maltese aristocracy in the burning of their patents of nobility during the French occupation. Three of his sons were selected for education in France, but he managed to buy them out. He was inside Valletta during the Siege. Sant had been a *Capitano della Verga* under the Order, then a lord lieutenant under Sir Alexander Ball to whom he would eventually present the Sword of Honour.

LUIGI SANT CASSIA, CMG, 8TH BARON GHARIEXEM AND TABIA AND 3RD COUNT SANT

He was the first of his line to use the name 'Sant Cassia'. He was renowned for his wealth, but his reputation was exaggerated. Luigi married Angela dei Marchesi Testaferrata Olivier. He quarrelled with his father who left much of the family wealth to his other sons, one of whom Publio Maria became bishop of Malta and kept a chapel in Palazzo Rocca Grande. His other brother Baldassare married Luigia Countess Fournier and started the 'Sant Fournier' line.

GIO' FRANCESCO SANT CASSIA 9TH BARON OF GHARIEXEM AND

TABIA AND 4TH COUNT SANT

He had an unhappy marriage, and his wife Giovanna Rosa Apap daughter of the 2nd Marquis of Ġnien is-Sultan left him and 'escaped' to Floriana.

GIOVANNI SANT CASSIA 10TH BARON OF GHARIEXEM AND TABIA AND 5TH COUNT SANT

He married a country girl by the name of Marianna Galea. He was a splendid Victorian eccentric. He would travel to Siġġiewi at night arriving at about 2 a.m. and demand a haircut for his son for which he paid a gold sovereign. An amiable and boisterous character, he was known to shoot wine bottles with the approval of publicans while stopping on his night rides. He always paid the bill. He was the owner of the Roman Villa and fought Count Strickland physically when it was acquisitioned in the public interest (Strickland was first secretary to the government). Sant Cassia bought Guarena Palace with the proceeds from the sale of Mtarfa Bridge to the government. Because of him, 1st class on the Malta train was divided into 'official' or 'otherwise'.

ALBERT V. LAFERLA,

LL.D. and his family lived in the house in the early years of the twentieth century. Laferla's diary covering the years 1906 and 1907 is an enlightening document and mentions Casa Rocca Piccola as the house in Valletta with a garden – an unusual feature.

FRANCESCO SANT CASSIA 11TH BARON OF GHARIEXEM AND TABIA AND 6TH COUNT SANT 1903

He was only 13 years old when he inherited his father. He was brought up by the Baroness Inguanez of Diar-il-Bniet and Bucana, doyenne of the Maltese Nobility. He was commissioned in the King's Own Malta Regiment of Militia. He married Maria Manduca and then, on her demise, her sister Concettina, both daughters of the Count of Mont'Alto. Cikku Sant, as he was known, was the father of 12 children. He entertained King George V to lunch at his house at St Paul's Bay. He was one of the first Maltese owner-drivers of a car and he even owned a bus. He left the island for Australia and returned. It was he who sold this house to the next owner.

COMMENDATORE ANTONIO CASSAR TORREGGIANI, OBE

He was the founder of The National Bank of Malta, and St George's Flour Mills, a senator, and a philanthropist. He commissioned the RMS *Knight of Malta* which, until she was requisitioned for war service, was the principal

passenger transport vessel to the Italian mainland. He was my maternal grandfather.

CHEVALIER JEROME DE PIRO D'AMICO INGUANEZ, KM, 8TH BARON OF BUDACH

(see section on The de Piro Family on page 31)

NICHOLAS 9TH MARQUIS DE PIRO AND 9TH BARON OF BUDACH 1990

(see section on The de Piro Family on page 31)

THE DE PIRO FAMILY

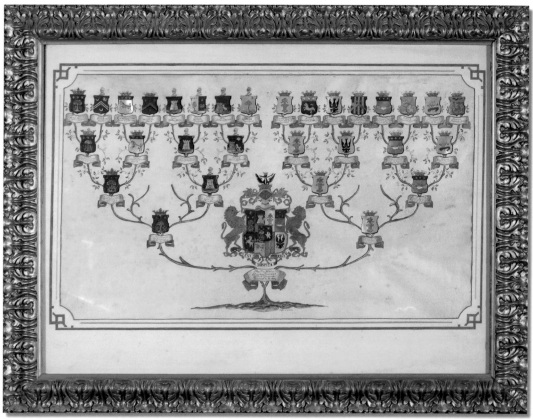

COSIMO de Piro, D'Epiro, or de Pyrrho whose family left Rhodes in the general exodus of the knights of St John, settled in Malta when the islands were granted to that brave Grand Master Fra Philippe Villiers de L'Isle Adam in 1530. He married Gerolama La Mattina. It is recorded that he was given trusted responsibility and made Commander of the Arsenal of the Sovereign Prince.

PAOLO, his second son, married Giovanella Albano and later Galizia Salemi. The second marriage produced:

LORENZO UBALDESCO, JUD *Juris Utriusque*

Lorenzo Ubaldesco de Piro

Doctor (meaning he was a doctor of both Civil and Canon law). His degree, an illuminated manuscript from the University of Messina, survives in the family archives and is dated 1668. He was appointed *uditore* to Grand Master Adrien de Wignacourt in 1694. He married Cornelia Cauchi and at her death took Holy Orders becoming a conventual chaplain of the knights and eventually archdeacon of the cathedral. He strove and eventually succeeded in procuring privileges for himself and his canons. By special decree, he was allowed not to be buried at St John's but in the cathedral instead. Pope

Clement XI allowed him, '… to totally abstain from presiding over executions and torture involving blood crimes …' He entailed his property in perpetuity in favour of his son the holder of the newly-granted title (1716) of Baron of Budach.

GIOVANNI PIO (Gio'Pio), JUD, 1st Baron of Budach and 1st Marquis de Piro 1673-1752 – He studied for his doctorate in Rome. He was appointed Ambassador representing the Grand Master and the *Università* as procurator of wheat. Grand Master Perellos created him Baron of Budach in 1716 with a tribute of two muskets to be paid on the feast of St Barbara every year. He became a *segreto* of the Inquisition in 1720 and in 1728 was curator of the Holy Office. He was placed in a position of further trust by being appointed *secreto* of Malta, Gozo, and Comino. His honours increased: he was appointed lieutenant of the regimental company to which the Grand Master's *famigliari* belonged. He was appointed *regio secreto* of Syracuse by the King of Spain.

Gio' Pio de Piro

By 1742 Gio'Pio was senior jurat of Valletta. As a stepping stone to his final accolade, he was temporally created Viscount Cartely but this title was suppressed in order to raise him further: on 6 November 1742 Philip V of Spain raised him to the rank of Marquis de Piro in the Kingdom of Castille.

Gio'Pio was an entrepreneur with seemingly insatiable ambition and unflagging energy. He was soon in charge of his family's business including the transactions involving infidel slaves. The family archives hold a bill for 1,500 scudi representing one transaction in which Gio'Pio is selling Muslims to a Muslim trader called Rais. But these were early days in his career, soon he would concentrate on other people's administrations and prove his reliability.

His marriage to Anna Antonia Gourgion considerably increased his worldly assets, and fortune seems to have been showered upon him for the rest of his life. His wealthy father-in-law's administration fell into his lap: Giovanni Gourgion was a landowner, Magistro di Sala of the Valletta magisterial palace and even a patron of Mattia Preti's. The artist painted both Giovanni and his wife pouring water over the Holy Souls in Purgatory in a great altarpiece at St George's Basilica in Gozo.

Gio'Pio's career was a triumph and perhaps the most successful of any Maltese man of his period. He invested in land, ships, and cargoes of textiles, grain, sugar, rice, and coffee. He would sometimes insure cargoes and ships on his own account. He

sometimes lent money, and quite often to knights of Malta including the illustrious Fra Carlo Albani, nephew of Clement XI.

Gio'Pio purchased land all over Malta and, in Sicily, great tracts in the plains of Girgenti. He kept houses in Valletta, in Mdina, by the sea in Scicli and also in the hexagonal city of Avola. He also invested in good unions. He married off his daughter to the Baron Ferdinando de Ribera and his granddaughter to Francesco, eldest son of the Duke of Montalto. Both ladies were given conspicuous dowries, the descriptions of which survive in the family archives.

His business affairs were administered with efficiency. The surviving papers including many of his letters make the point. He was always aware of what was happening and crosschecked his information through a series of agents in Malta, Sicily, Naples, and Rome. He organised the education of his sons through his contacts: Angelo went to Siena and was made to take Holy Orders against his will; Felicissimo Antonio went to Lyons and he predeceased his father; Vincenzo, his adored grandson and heir, went to Rome, under the tutelage of the Albani family.

Gio'Pio was conscientious and even religious. He endowed charities: he helped spinsters, and donated altars and embellishments, he gave oil and legacies for masses to churches. He died in 1752 after his son, and was succeeded by his grandson. He is buried with his wife in his family vault under an *intarsio* marble tombstone in the main aisle of St Francis Church in Valletta.

ANTONIO FELICISSIMO, Baroncino of Budach and Marchesino de Piro, died before his father. He was secreto to Grand Master Despuig. He married Elena Grech Balzani as his third wife in 1736 and died in 1739. From this

final union was born a son and heir.

VINCENZO, 2nd Baron of Budach and 2nd Marquis de Piro 1736-99. He became a jurat and also procurator of the Inquisition. He was interested in military tactics and operations and was appointed Colonel of the Royal Sicilian Regiment. He helped to raise the rebellion against the French invaders, and was elected one of the four representatives of the people. He had married Maria Testaferrata Abela, daughter of the 3rd Baron of Gomerino in 1757. He died in 1799 having nominated his eldest son Antonio to the barony and his second son Giuseppe to the marquisate. ANTONIO, the 3rd Baron of Budach 1758-1806, was not left the marquisate because of his liaison with

one Maria Teresa Speranza Campanella de lo Re. They produced children out of wedlock, two of whom took Holy Orders. The couple eventually married and were blessed with a legitimate scholarly and erudite heir. SIR GIUSEPPE MARIA, GCMG, 4th Baron of Budach, 1794-1870. He was the author of *A History of the*

him first Maltese captain commandant of the Malta Militia. He died without legitimate heirs in 1870 and was succeeded by his sister.

FRANCESCA, 5th Baroness of Budach, was a spinster. She inherited her brother and died seven years later in 1877. She attempted to leave her title and estates to the Bishop of Gozo. Following a successful claim in the courts by Guiseppe de Piro he succeeded her. Giuseppe was the eldest son of her deceased first cousin Carmelo.

GIUSEPPE (Pinu), 6th Baron of Budach 1845-1916, was a bachelor, a keen gardener, and enthusiastic builder and lover of ceremonial. He was a Knight of Cape and Sword at the Vatican. He devoted his energies to building some noteworthy follies, among them a villa in Rome, a neo-Gothic house in Mdina, and, perhaps, he created the finest garden in Malta attached to his Villa Gourgion in Lija. He allowed his cousins the Marquises Francesco Xaverio and Giuseppe Lorenzo to use the title and indeed even enjoy some of the patrimony; his law-suit over

Plague of 1813 and *Pieces of History* (both written in Italian). The second book was an impassioned answer to Adolphus Slade's vitriolic and denigrating commentary on Malta. In his book he listed Maltese savants and artists together with their creditable works of merit. He set out to prove that his compatriots had been the principal factors in procuring their emancipation and had voluntarily submitted to England's help. It should be remembered that England did not lose a single soldier in the procurement of Malta.

According to William Hardman's *A History of Malta during the Period of the French and British Occupations 1798-1815*, Sir Giuseppe Maria was an aspirant to the government of the islands (p. 643). He married the wealthy Antonia Moscati Gatto Xara, 3rd Baroness of Benwarrad and widow of Sir Paolo Parisio, GCMG. They lived in the magnificent Palazzo Parisio where Napoleon had chosen to spend his days in Malta. Giuseppe Maria presented the famous 'Majmuna Stone' (now in the Gozo Museum) to the nation. Governor Reid historically appointed

the inheritance of Francesca had established him as the senior de Piro heir and he had no desire to upset his cousins. His own heir was not his younger brother (my great-grandfather Alessandro, 1849-99) because Alessandro died first.

Alessandro had married the heiress Orsola Agius Caruana and she brought a great palazzo in Florence into the family. It had been the seat of the Florentine commandery and embassy of the Knights of Malta in the days of the Grand Duchy of Tuscany. One of their seven sons, Monsignor Giuseppe de Piro, founded the Missionary Society of St Paul and is now a strong candidate for beatification. Pinu's heirs were his nephews Igino who inherited his titles and the entails of the barony of Budach and of the marquisate and his younger brother Pio who inherited the large Gourgion estates.

IGINO 1874-1942 7th Baron of Budach. Educated at the Lyceum and the Royal University of Malta. He married my grandmother Nicolina, daughter of Felicissimo Apap Bologna, 4th Marquis of Gnien-is-Sultan. He fought in the Boer War and was present at the Siege of Ladysmith (Queen's Medal three clasps). He was Adjutant for five years

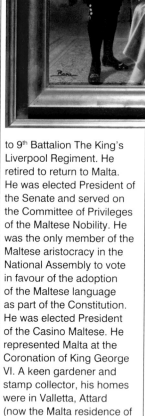

to 9th Battalion The King's Liverpool Regiment. He retired to return to Malta. He was elected President of the Senate and served on the Committee of Privileges of the Maltese Nobility. He was the only member of the Maltese aristocracy in the National Assembly to vote in favour of the adoption of the Maltese language as part of the Constitution. He was elected President of the Casino Maltese. He represented Malta at the Coronation of King George VI. A keen gardener and stamp collector, his homes were in Valletta, Attard (now the Malta residence of Grand Master Fra Andrew Bertie), St Paul's Bay, and Florence. His heir was his only son.

JEROME, 8th Baron of Budach my father 1914-96. Educated at Collège Champittet, Lausanne, Switzerland. He served as a gunner in World War II in the 2nd A.A. Regiment of the Royal Malta Artillery (Africa Star, 1939-45 Star, War Medal 1939-45, Victory Medal). He had been a member of the Committee of Privileges of the Maltese Nobility for 40 years and, for a long period, its president. On his retirement, he was elected President of the Committee of Privileges Emeritus ad vitam. Jerome represented the Maltese nobility in the National Congress and in the National Assembly; also, with my mother at the Coronation of Queen Elizabeth II. He was a Knight of Honour and Devotion of the Sovereign Military Order of Malta. He married Phyllis Cassar Torreggiani and they had 5 children: Nicholas, Madeleine, Mary, Elizabeth, and Margaret.

NICHOLAS, born 1941, 9th and present Marquis de Piro and Baron of Budach. Married Frances Elizabeth

Wilson on 1 October 1970 and has issue: Cosmo, Clement, Louisa, and Anton. The family lived at Painswick House in Gloucestershire for 14 years before returning to Malta. Nicholas is the author of 6 books: *Lost Letters* (with Kenneth Zammit Tabona and others; Pedigree Books London), *The International Dictionary of Artists who Painted Malta; Picking Through The Stones*, and *Notions, Nostalgia and Nonsense Poems* (both Said International, Malta); *Valletta; Mdina; The Temple of the Knights of Malta* (Miranda Publications, with photos by Daniel Cilia); *Costume in Malta* (with Vicki Ann Cremona). At the time of going to press, there are three grandchildren, Serafina, Nicholas and Mary Bene-dicta.

GIUSEPPE, 3rd Marquis de Piro d. 1852 was the second son of Vincenzo de Piro and also inherited the great Gourgion estates. His older brother Antonio inherited the barony of Budach. From 15 September 1799 to 8 September 1800 Giuseppe was captain of the insurgent and heroic troops called Cacciatori Maltesi. Under British rule he became colonel of the Royal Malta Fencible Regiment and completed 47 years and 194 days service. A document dated 1888 declares that during the siege of Valletta, 'Col. The Marquis Giuseppe de Piro, CMG was always selected by his colleagues to convey personally the dispatches to Lord Nelson'. His eldest son succeeded him.

ADRIANO, 4th Marquis de Piro 1817-66, died unmarried, and the next in line was his brother my great-great-grandfather Dr Carmelo de Piro, MD. 1820-69. However, it was his younger brother who was nominated.

FRANCESCO XAVERIO, 5th Marquis de Piro 1824-94, married Adelaide Testaferrata, daughter of 5th Marquis Cassar Desain. He was a member of the Council of Government; sometime president of the Committee of Privileges of the Maltese Nobility; lieutenant colonel commanding the Royal Malta Fencible Artillery. He retired in the rank of colonel in 1884.

GIUSEPPE LORENZO, 6th Marquis de Piro, was born in 1858 and was educated at Stonyhurst College. He was made CMG on the occasion of Queen Victoria's Golden Jubilee. He was chamberlain to Pope Leo XIII; ADC to the governor of Malta; knight of Malta; lieutenant colonel commanding the 1st Battalion of the Royal Malta Militia. He became a legend in the Mess owing to his gourmandish proclivity and capacity. His brass bed was so enormous that on one occasion when it was moved to his summer residence it was mistaken for a bandstand. He was succeeded by his only daughter.

ADELINA VICTORIA, 7th Marchioness de Piro in her own right 1892-1962. She was a renowned beauty and married Kenneth MacPherson. They lived in Lija and Monaco and produced no heirs.

JEROME – Adelina's cousin – born 1914 was recognized as 8th Marquis de Piro by the Committee of Privileges of the Maltese Nobility. He relinquished his title in favour of his only son by special permission of the said Committee. (see biography on opposite page)

NICHOLAS, born 1941, 9th and present Marquis de Piro and Baron of Budach. (see biography above)

The Maltese Lady c 1760 by Francesco Zahra